■ **SCHOLASTIC**

MW00594358

Success With

Fractions & Decimals

New York • Toronto • London • Auckland • Sydney
Mexico City • New Delhi • Hong Kong • Buenos Aires

Teaching *Resources*

State Standards Correlations

To find out how this book helps you meet your state's standards, log on to **www.scholastic.com/ssw**

Written by William Earl
Cover design by Ka-Yeon Kim-Li
Interior illustrations by Don O'Connor
Interior design by Quack & Company

ISBN 978-0-545-20089-9

11 12 13 14 15 16 17 18   40   20 19 18

Introduction

Parents and teachers alike will find this book to be a valuable learning tool. Students will enjoy completing a wide variety of math activities as they learn about fractions and decimals. The activities are both engaging and educational. Take a look at the Table of Contents and you will feel rewarded providing such a valuable resource for your students. Remember to praise them for their efforts and successes!

Table of Contents

Jumping Lily Pads!

A fraction consists of two parts.

 $\dfrac{5}{}$

The **numerator** *tells how many parts are being identified.*

 $\overline{6}$ $= \dfrac{5}{6}$

The **denominator** *tells how many equal parts there are.*

Identify the fraction of the shaded part for each lily pad.

💡 **There were 9 lily pads on the pond. On 4 of the lily pads, sat a frog. On another sheet of paper, draw a picture to show this fractional set.**

Let's Split It Up

 To find the fractional part of a number, follow these steps.

$\frac{3}{4}$ of 12

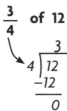

$3 \times 3 = 9$

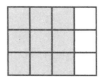

1. Divide the whole number by the denominator.

2. Multiply the quotient by the numerator.

$\frac{3}{4}$ of 12 = 9

Find the fractional part of each whole number. Shade each box to show the answer.

A. $\frac{1}{3}$ of 9 = —

$\frac{1}{4}$ of 8 = —

$\frac{1}{6}$ of 12 = —

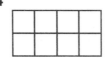

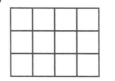

Find the fractional part of each number.

B. $\frac{1}{5}$ of 10 = — $\frac{1}{8}$ of 16 = — $\frac{3}{5}$ of 15 = —

C. $\frac{3}{4}$ of 20 = — $\frac{5}{6}$ of 30 = — $\frac{3}{7}$ of 14 = —

D. $\frac{6}{8}$ of 32 = — $\frac{2}{9}$ of 18 = — $\frac{1}{2}$ of 20 = —

E. $\frac{1}{6}$ of 18 = — $\frac{1}{8}$ of 40 = — $\frac{1}{7}$ of 21 = —

 Mrs. Baker found 25 shells on the beach. She brought 2/5 of the shells to her classroom. The rest of the shells she set on a bookshelf at her house. How many shells did she bring to school? How many shells are at her house? (Show your work on another sheet of paper if necessary.)

You Call That Equal?

 Equivalent fractions *have the same amount.*

$$\frac{1}{2} = \frac{}{8}$$

Equivalent fractions are the same amount of pizza, with simply different size slices!

$$\frac{1 \times 4}{2 \times 4} = \frac{4}{8}$$

What times 2 equals 8? 4! Then multiply the numerator by 4.

 $\frac{1}{2}$ $\frac{2}{4}$ $\frac{3}{6}$ $\frac{4}{8}$

Write the equivalent fractions.

A.

____ = ____   ____ = ____   ____ = ____   ____ = ____

Find each equivalent fraction.

B. $\frac{2}{7} = \frac{}{21}$ $\frac{3}{6} = \frac{}{12}$ $\frac{3}{4} = \frac{}{8}$ $\frac{3}{7} = \frac{}{14}$

C. $\frac{5}{6} = \frac{}{36}$ $\frac{5}{8} = \frac{}{16}$ $\frac{2}{6} = \frac{}{36}$ $\frac{3}{7} = \frac{}{49}$

D. $\frac{3}{4} = \frac{12}{}$ $\frac{7}{9} = \frac{21}{}$ $\frac{5}{9} = \frac{}{27}$ $\frac{7}{10} = \frac{}{100}$

Name _____

Let's Climb to the Top!

 Multiples of a number can be found by multiplying that number by 0, 1, 2, 3, 4, . . .
The multiples of 3 are 0, 3, 6, 9, 12, . . .

The **least common multiple (LCM)** of two numbers is the least number other than 0 that is a multiple of each. To find the least common multiple of two numbers, find the multiples of each number.

Multiples of 3: 0, 3, 6, 9, 12, 15
Multiples of 4: 0, 4, 8, 12, 16, 20

The first multiple after 0 that is the same is 12. The LCM is 12.

Find the least common multiple for each set of numbers.

4, 7 = ____

3, 6 = ____

2, 5 = ____

3, 5 = ____

2, 3 = ____

4, 5 = ____

5, 6 = ____

2, 4 = ____

2, 7 = ____

3, 7 = ____

4, 6 = ____

4, 8 = ____

2, 8 = ____

3, 8 = ____

5, 7 = ____

5, 8 = ____

2, 10 = ____

4, 12 = ____

5, 10 = ____

2, 9 = ____

3, 9 = ____

6, 8 = ____

6, 7 = ____

4, 9 = ____

3, 4 = ____

8, 10 = ____

4, 10 = ____

 **Start!**

You made it!

Ready to Reduce

The **greatest common factor** *(GCF)* of two numbers is the greatest number that is a factor of each. To reduce a fraction to lowest terms, follow these steps.

$$\frac{8}{12} \qquad\qquad \frac{8 \div 4}{12 \div 4} = \frac{2}{3} \qquad\qquad \frac{2}{3}$$

1. *Find the greatest common factor.*

   Factors of 8 = 1, 2, 4, 8

   Factors of 12 = 1, 2, 3, 4, 6, 12

   The GCF = 4

2. *Divide the numerator and the denominator by the GCF.*

3. *Since 2 and 3 have no common factors other than 1, the fraction is in lowest terms.*

Write the factors for the numerator and denominator. Circle the greatest common factor.

A. Factors of 5:_____

   Factors of 15: _____

B. Factors of 6: _____

   Factors of 18: _____

C. Factors of 3:_____

   Factors of 21: _____

D. Factors of 7: _____

   Factors of 28: _____

Find the GCF. Reduce.

E. $\dfrac{4}{10} \begin{array}{c}\div\\\div\end{array}$ = ___ $\dfrac{6}{12} \begin{array}{c}\div\\\div\end{array}$ = ___ $\dfrac{3}{12} \begin{array}{c}\div\\\div\end{array}$ = ___

F. $\dfrac{4}{20} \begin{array}{c}\div\\\div\end{array}$ = ___ $\dfrac{3}{21} \begin{array}{c}\div\\\div\end{array}$ = ___ $\dfrac{5}{15} \begin{array}{c}\div\\\div\end{array}$ = ___

G. $\dfrac{7}{21} \begin{array}{c}\div\\\div\end{array}$ = ___ $\dfrac{3}{24} \begin{array}{c}\div\\\div\end{array}$ = ___ $\dfrac{7}{28} \begin{array}{c}\div\\\div\end{array}$ = ___

Write the numbers 1–30 each on a card. Draw two cards. Find the greatest common factor for the two numbers. Continue until you have used all the cards.

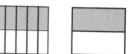

It's Time to Reduce

 A fraction is in **lowest terms** *if the numerator and denominator have no common factors other than one. To reduce a fraction to lowest terms, follow these steps.*

$$\frac{5}{10}$$

$$\frac{5}{10} \begin{array}{c} \div 5 \\ \div 5 \end{array} = \frac{1}{2}$$

1. Find the GCF for 5 and 10.

2. Divide.

$$\frac{5}{10} = \frac{1}{2}$$

Shade each space with a fraction in lowest terms blue. Shade each space with a fraction not in lowest terms yellow.

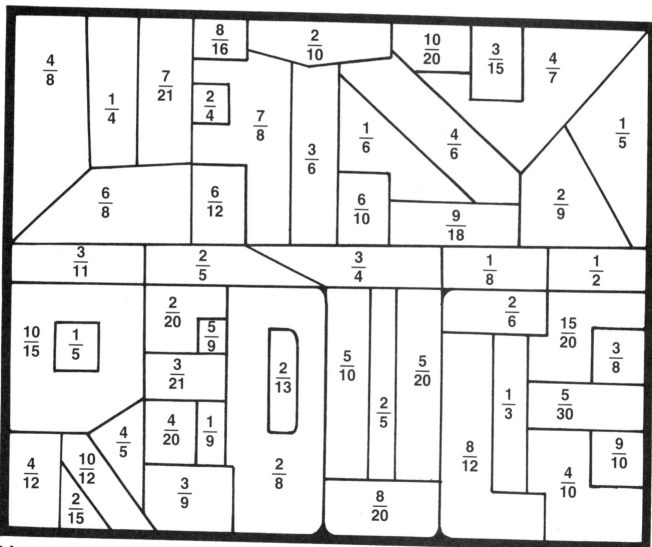

 On another sheet of paper, reduce each fraction shaded yellow.

Which Way Did He Go?

 To compare fractions, first look at the denominators. If the denominators are different, follow these steps.

$$\frac{2}{3}$$

$$\frac{5}{6}$$

$$\frac{2}{3} = \frac{4}{6}$$

$$\frac{5}{6} = \frac{5}{6}$$

$$\frac{4}{6} < \frac{5}{6}$$

1. Find the LCM for the denominators.

2. Use the LCM to make equivalent fractions with a common denominator.

3. Compare.

Write >, or <, or = to compare each set of fractions.

A. $\frac{1}{2}$ ◯ $\frac{3}{4}$ $\frac{5}{6}$ ◯ $\frac{10}{12}$ $\frac{3}{8}$ ◯ $\frac{1}{16}$ $\frac{3}{10}$ ◯ $\frac{4}{5}$

B. $\frac{3}{7}$ ◯ $\frac{1}{14}$ $\frac{6}{8}$ ◯ $\frac{1}{4}$ $\frac{4}{6}$ ◯ $\frac{4}{18}$ $\frac{8}{12}$ ◯ $\frac{2}{3}$

C. $\frac{4}{7}$ ◯ $\frac{4}{21}$ $\frac{5}{11}$ ◯ $\frac{5}{22}$ $\frac{8}{9}$ ◯ $\frac{2}{18}$ $\frac{7}{8}$ ◯ $\frac{7}{24}$

 Kendall saw two deer in the forest. He quietly watched as each ate a twig from a tree. When Kendall moved closer, the deer heard him and scampered away. Kendall determined that one deer had eaten 6/8 of a twig and the other 3/4 of a twig. Which deer had eaten the most?

Name _____

Howling Fun

 To change an improper fraction to a mixed number, follow these steps.

$$\frac{13}{6} \qquad 6\overline{\smash{\big)}13} \atop \quad \underline{-12} \atop \qquad 1 \quad \overset{2}{}$$

$$6\overline{\smash{\big)}13} \atop \quad \underline{-12} \atop \qquad 1 \quad \overset{2\ R1}{} = 2\frac{1}{6}$$

$$\frac{12}{6} \qquad 6\overline{\smash{\big)}12} \atop \quad \underline{-12} \atop \qquad 0 \quad \overset{2}{}$$

1. *Divide the denominator into the numerator.*

2. *The remainder becomes the numerator. The divisor becomes the denominator.*

3. *If there is no remainder, the improper fraction becomes a whole number.*

Change each improper fraction to a mixed or whole number.
Then use the code to answer the question below.

A. $\frac{18}{7}$ =	H. $\frac{19}{7}$ =	S. $\frac{18}{9}$ =
B. $\frac{28}{7}$ =	I. $\frac{14}{3}$ =	T. $\frac{7}{4}$ =
C. $\frac{19}{5}$ =	K. $\frac{17}{4}$ =	U. $\frac{20}{6}$ =
E. $\frac{15}{4}$ =	R. $\frac{30}{4}$ =	W. $\frac{11}{5}$ =

Why did the dog howl?

$$\overline{\quad 4 \quad} \quad \overline{\ 3\frac{3}{4}\ } \quad \overline{\ 3\frac{4}{5}\ } \quad \overline{\ 2\frac{4}{7}\ } \quad \overline{\ 3\frac{2}{6}\ } \quad \overline{\quad 2 \quad} \quad \overline{\ 3\frac{3}{4}\ }$$

$$\overline{\ 4\frac{2}{3}\ } \quad \overline{\ 1\frac{3}{4}\ } \qquad\qquad \overline{\quad 2 \quad} \quad \overline{\ 2\frac{4}{7}\ } \quad \overline{\ 2\frac{1}{5}\ }$$

$$\overline{\ 1\frac{3}{4}\ } \quad \overline{\ 2\frac{5}{7}\ } \quad \overline{\ 3\frac{3}{4}\ }$$

$$\overline{\ 1\frac{3}{4}\ } \quad \overline{\ 7\frac{2}{4}\ } \quad \overline{\ 3\frac{3}{4}\ } \quad \overline{\ 3\frac{3}{4}\ }$$

$$\overline{\quad 4 \quad} \quad \overline{\ 2\frac{4}{7}\ } \quad \overline{\ 7\frac{2}{4}\ } \quad \overline{\ 4\frac{1}{4}\ }$$

An Ocean of Fun

 To change a mixed number to an improper fraction, follow these steps.

$3\frac{1}{5}$ $3 \times 5 = 15$

$15 + 1 = 16$

$3\frac{1}{5} = \frac{16}{5}$

1. Multiply the whole number and denominator.

2. Add the numerator to the product.

3. Place this sum over the denominator.

Change each mixed number to an improper fraction.

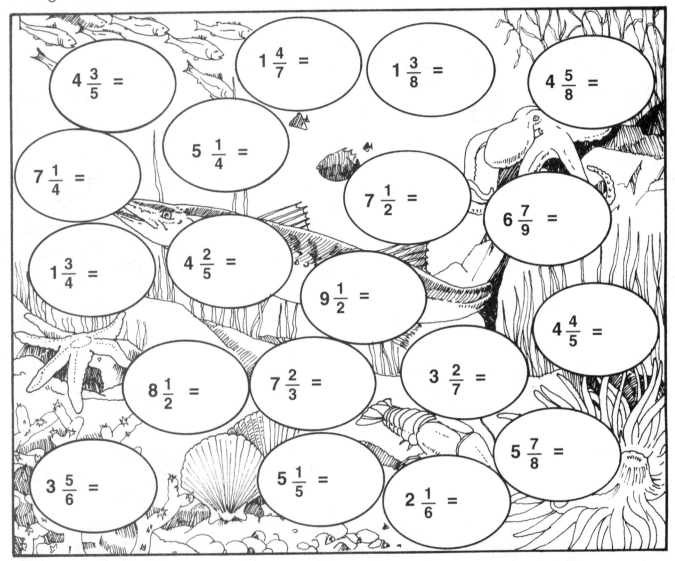

$4\frac{3}{5} =$ $1\frac{4}{7} =$ $1\frac{3}{8} =$ $4\frac{5}{8} =$

$5\frac{1}{4} =$

$7\frac{1}{4} =$ $7\frac{1}{2} =$ $6\frac{7}{9} =$

$1\frac{3}{4} =$ $4\frac{2}{5} =$

$9\frac{1}{2} =$ $4\frac{4}{5} =$

$8\frac{1}{2} =$ $7\frac{2}{3} =$ $3\frac{2}{7} =$

$5\frac{7}{8} =$

$3\frac{5}{6} =$ $5\frac{1}{5} =$ $2\frac{1}{6} =$

 While scuba diving in the ocean, Joe and his dad discovered a treasure chest. Inside the chest were hundreds of coins. They brought the chest back to their boat. Joe sorted the coins. He counted 12 whole gold-trimmed silver coins. There was also 3/4 of another coin of the same type. Write an improper fraction for the number of gold-trimmed silver coins.

Name _____

Yea or Neigh?

 To add fractions with the same denominator, follow these steps

$\frac{3}{8} + \frac{3}{8} = \frac{6}{}$ $\frac{3}{8} + \frac{3}{8} = \frac{6}{8}$ $\frac{6}{8} = \frac{3}{4}$

1. Add the numerators.   2. The denominators remain the same.   3. Reduce to lowest terms.

What's the difference between kids and horses when it comes to voting on whether to have spaghetti for dinner?

Add. Then use the code below to answer the riddle. Remember to reduce to lowest terms.

$\frac{3}{7} + \frac{2}{7}$ $\frac{6}{12} + \frac{3}{12}$ $\frac{5}{8} + \frac{2}{8}$ $\frac{2}{4} + \frac{3}{4}$ $\frac{3}{16} + \frac{4}{16}$

$\frac{7}{9} + \frac{1}{9}$ $\frac{3}{8} + \frac{1}{8}$ $\frac{7}{12} + \frac{6}{12}$ $\frac{5}{6} + \frac{2}{6}$ $\frac{3}{6} + \frac{1}{6}$

$\frac{3}{20} + \frac{4}{20}$ $\frac{6}{5} + \frac{1}{5}$ $\frac{5}{4} + \frac{3}{4}$ $\frac{10}{5} + \frac{16}{5}$ $\frac{5}{8} + \frac{7}{8}$

$\frac{4}{9} + \frac{1}{9}$ $\frac{4}{2} + \frac{4}{2}$ $\frac{3}{11} + \frac{4}{11}$

on = $5\frac{1}{5}$	Kids = $\frac{5}{7}$	They'd = $1\frac{1}{12}$	munching = $\frac{7}{20}$
will = $\frac{3}{4}$	be = $\frac{2}{3}$	oats = $1\frac{1}{2}$	crunching = 2
yea = $1\frac{1}{4}$	and = $\frac{7}{16}$	rather = $1\frac{1}{6}$	! = $\frac{7}{11}$
and = $1\frac{2}{5}$	and = $\frac{5}{9}$	neigh (nay)! = $\frac{1}{2}$	horses = $\frac{8}{9}$
vote = $\frac{7}{8}$	hay = 4		

Fraction Tic-Tac-Toe

To add fractions with unlike denominators, follow these steps.

$$\dfrac{1}{3} = \dfrac{}{6}$$
$$+\dfrac{2}{6} = \dfrac{}{6}$$

1. Find the common denominator.

$$\dfrac{1}{3} = \dfrac{2}{6}$$
$$\dfrac{2}{6} = \dfrac{2}{6}$$

2. Find equivalent fractions.

$$\dfrac{2}{6}$$
$$+\dfrac{2}{6}$$
$$\dfrac{4}{6}$$

3. Add.

$$\dfrac{4 \div 2}{6 \div 2} = \dfrac{2}{3}$$

4. Reduce to lowest terms.

Add. Reduce to lowest terms. Then use the Key to fill in the X's and O's.

Key

$\dfrac{3}{5} = O$	$\dfrac{7}{8} = X$
$\dfrac{4}{5} = O$	$\dfrac{1}{4} = O$
$\dfrac{4}{15} = O$	$\dfrac{5}{12} = X$
$\dfrac{4}{9} = X$	$\dfrac{7}{9} = O$
$\dfrac{3}{14} = X$	$\dfrac{1}{2} = X$
$\dfrac{3}{8} = X$	$\dfrac{3}{10} = X$
$\dfrac{2}{3} = O$	$\dfrac{7}{12} = O$
$\dfrac{5}{8} = X$	$\dfrac{5}{6} = X$
$\dfrac{3}{4} = X$	$1 = O$
$\dfrac{7}{16} = X$	

A.

$+\dfrac{1}{2}\ \dfrac{1}{8}$	$+\dfrac{1}{2}\ \dfrac{1}{4}$	$+\dfrac{1}{6}\ \dfrac{1}{2}$
$+\dfrac{1}{4}\ \dfrac{1}{8}$	$+\dfrac{1}{5}\ \dfrac{1}{10}$	$+\dfrac{1}{3}\ \dfrac{1}{6}$
$+\dfrac{1}{2}\ \dfrac{1}{10}$	$+\dfrac{1}{5}\ \dfrac{1}{15}$	$+\dfrac{1}{3}\ \dfrac{1}{9}$

B.

$+\dfrac{1}{4}\ \dfrac{5}{8}$	$+\dfrac{1}{6}\ \dfrac{1}{12}$	$+\dfrac{1}{3}\ \dfrac{1}{12}$
$+\dfrac{2}{3}\ \dfrac{2}{6}$	$+\dfrac{1}{2}\ \dfrac{1}{12}$	$+\dfrac{1}{2}\ \dfrac{2}{6}$
$+\dfrac{1}{7}\ \dfrac{1}{14}$	$+\dfrac{3}{16}\ \dfrac{1}{4}$	$+\dfrac{2}{3}\ \dfrac{1}{9}$

Name _____

Hold On!

Add. Change improper fractions to mixed numbers. Reduce to lowest terms. Then use the code to answer the riddle below.

O.
$$\frac{1}{2} + \frac{1}{3}$$

W.
$$\frac{1}{4} + \frac{1}{3}$$

E.
$$\frac{1}{5} + \frac{1}{2}$$

G.
$$\frac{2}{3} + \frac{1}{7}$$

S.
$$\frac{4}{5} + \frac{2}{3}$$

A.
$$\frac{1}{3} + \frac{3}{9}$$

L.
$$\frac{1}{4} + \frac{1}{7}$$

O.
$$\frac{2}{5} + \frac{1}{3}$$

I.
$$\frac{3}{4} + \frac{4}{5}$$

N.
$$\frac{2}{9} + \frac{1}{2}$$

R.
$$\frac{3}{5} + \frac{1}{4}$$

D.
$$\frac{2}{4} + \frac{4}{6}$$

H.
$$\frac{5}{8} + \frac{3}{5}$$

!
$$\frac{2}{6} + \frac{1}{5}$$

U.
$$\frac{3}{8} + \frac{2}{7}$$

N.
$$\frac{3}{6} + \frac{1}{4}$$

Y.
$$\frac{3}{7} + \frac{1}{4}$$

Why was the cowboy a lot of laughs?

___ ___   ___ ___ ___   ___ ___ ___ ___ ___ ___
$1\frac{9}{40}$ $\frac{7}{10}$ $\frac{7}{12}$ $\frac{2}{3}$ $1\frac{7}{15}$ $\frac{2}{3}$ $\frac{11}{28}$ $\frac{7}{12}$ $\frac{2}{3}$ $\frac{19}{28}$ $1\frac{7}{15}$

___ ___ ___ ___ ___ ___ ___   ___ ___ ___ ___ ___ ___ ___
$1\frac{9}{40}$ $\frac{5}{6}$ $\frac{17}{20}$ $1\frac{7}{15}$ $1\frac{11}{20}$ $\frac{3}{4}$ $\frac{17}{21}$ $\frac{2}{3}$ $\frac{17}{20}$ $\frac{11}{15}$ $\frac{37}{56}$ $\frac{13}{18}$ $1\frac{1}{6}$ $\frac{8}{15}$

The Rapids Are Approaching!

To add mixed numbers, follow these steps.

$$1\frac{2}{4} = \frac{4}{8}$$
$$+\ 1\frac{6}{8} = \frac{6}{8}$$

$$1\frac{4}{8}$$
$$+\ 1\frac{6}{8}$$
$$\overline{\frac{10}{8}} = 1\frac{2}{8}$$

2. Add the fractions. Change the improper fraction to a mixed number.

$$\overset{1}{1}\frac{4}{8}$$
$$+\ 1\frac{6}{8}$$
$$\overline{3\frac{2}{8}}$$

$$3\frac{1}{4}$$

1. Find equivalent fractions.

3. Add the whole numbers.

4. Reduce the fraction to lowest terms.

Add. Reduce to lowest terms.

A.

$$1\frac{1}{2}$$
$$+\ 3\frac{1}{8}$$

$$4\frac{1}{2}$$
$$+\ 2\frac{4}{6}$$

$$3\frac{1}{2}$$
$$+\ 1\frac{3}{4}$$

B.

$$2\frac{3}{7}$$
$$+\ 1\frac{1}{14}$$

$$3\frac{1}{6}$$
$$+\ \ \frac{1}{2}$$

$$1\frac{1}{2}$$
$$+\ 2\frac{1}{3}$$

C.

$$4\frac{2}{3}$$
$$+\ 3\frac{1}{6}$$

$$3\frac{5}{8}$$
$$+\ 1\frac{4}{8}$$

$$4\frac{1}{6}$$
$$+\ 1\frac{1}{2}$$

$$5\frac{3}{9}$$
$$+\ 1\frac{1}{3}$$

D.

$$6\frac{1}{3}$$
$$+\ \ \frac{2}{6}$$

$$3\frac{1}{3}$$
$$+\ \ \frac{4}{9}$$

$$6\frac{1}{2}$$
$$+\ 2\frac{4}{6}$$

$$1\frac{1}{4}$$
$$+\ 3\frac{7}{8}$$

E.

$$2\frac{3}{5}$$
$$+\ 1\frac{1}{4}$$

$$3\frac{2}{4}$$
$$+\ 1\frac{1}{8}$$

$$9\frac{2}{5}$$
$$+\ \ \frac{8}{10}$$

$$\frac{4}{5}$$
$$+\ 3\frac{9}{10}$$

Laura and her brother went canoeing down the Snake River. They paddled for 2 and 3/4 hours before stopping for lunch. After lunch, they paddled for 3 and 4/8 hours. How long did they paddle altogether?

Name _____

A Grand Canyon

 To subtract fractions with unlike denominators, follow these steps.

$$\frac{3}{4} = \frac{}{8}$$
$$-\frac{4}{8} = \frac{}{8}$$

1. Find the least common denominator.

$$\frac{3 \times 2}{4 \times 2} = \frac{6}{8}$$
$$- \quad \frac{4}{8}$$

2. Find equivalent fractions.

$$\frac{6}{8}$$
$$-\frac{4}{8}$$
$$\frac{2}{8}$$

3. Subtract.

$$\frac{2}{8} = \frac{1}{4}$$

4. Reduce to lowest terms.

Subtract. Reduce to lowest terms. Then write the numerator of the problems listed below to complete the interesting fact.

A. $\frac{7}{14} - \frac{3}{7}$

B. $\frac{4}{5} - \frac{10}{15}$

C. $\frac{4}{6} - \frac{5}{12}$

D. $\frac{2}{3} - \frac{1}{12}$

E. $\frac{4}{7} - \frac{7}{14}$

F. $\frac{23}{25} - \frac{3}{5}$

G. $\frac{4}{8} - \frac{4}{16}$

H. $\frac{7}{10} - \frac{3}{5}$

I. $\frac{2}{3} - \frac{4}{9}$

J. $\frac{5}{6} - \frac{3}{12}$

K. $\frac{3}{4} - \frac{8}{12}$

L. $\frac{9}{10} - \frac{3}{5}$

M. $\frac{4}{7} - \frac{3}{14}$

N. $\frac{7}{9} - \frac{3}{18}$

O. $\frac{4}{5} - \frac{6}{15}$

Grand Canyon National Park covers

____ , ____ ____ ____ , ____ ____ ____ **acres.**
  K   I   C   F   L   D   M

Name _____

Sailing Through Subtraction

Subtract. Reduce to lowest terms.

A. $\frac{4}{5}$ $-\frac{1}{2}$ $\frac{7}{8}$ $-\frac{2}{3}$ $\frac{1}{2}$ $-\frac{1}{3}$ $\frac{1}{3}$ $-\frac{1}{4}$

B. $\frac{3}{6}$ $-\frac{1}{5}$ $\frac{4}{5}$ $-\frac{1}{3}$ $\frac{6}{8}$ $-\frac{1}{3}$ $\frac{3}{4}$ $-\frac{1}{5}$

C. $\frac{6}{7}$ $-\frac{1}{4}$ $\frac{4}{5}$ $-\frac{1}{6}$ $\frac{1}{2}$ $-\frac{1}{9}$ $\frac{2}{3}$ $-\frac{1}{2}$

D. $\frac{3}{7}$ $-\frac{2}{5}$ $\frac{4}{7}$ $-\frac{1}{2}$ $\frac{7}{8}$ $-\frac{1}{3}$ $\frac{2}{3}$ $-\frac{2}{5}$

E. $\frac{5}{8}$ $-\frac{1}{5}$ $\frac{2}{3}$ $-\frac{1}{7}$ $\frac{8}{9}$ $-\frac{1}{2}$ $\frac{4}{5}$ $-\frac{2}{3}$

Sliding Through Subtraction

 To subtract mixed numbers, follow these steps.

$$3\frac{2}{3} = \frac{8}{12}$$
$$-2\frac{2}{4} = \frac{6}{12}$$

1. Find the least common denominator. Then find equivalent fractions.

$$3\frac{8}{12}$$
$$-2\frac{6}{12}$$
$$\overline{\frac{2}{12}}$$

2. Subtract the fractions.

$$3\frac{8}{12}$$
$$-2\frac{6}{12}$$
$$\overline{1\frac{2}{12} = 1\frac{1}{6}}$$

3. Subtract the whole numbers. Reduce to lowest terms.

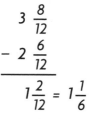

Subtract. Reduce to lowest terms.

A.

$6\frac{3}{5}$ $4\frac{6}{7}$ $5\frac{4}{5}$ $3\frac{4}{6}$
$-3\frac{1}{5}$ $-3\frac{5}{7}$ $-3\frac{3}{5}$ $-2\frac{3}{6}$

B.

$7\frac{5}{9}$ $8\frac{3}{4}$ $5\frac{7}{8}$ $9\frac{9}{10}$ $4\frac{7}{11}$
$-3\frac{2}{9}$ $-4\frac{1}{4}$ $-3\frac{5}{8}$ $-6\frac{6}{10}$ $-3\frac{4}{11}$

C.

$5\frac{2}{3}$ $5\frac{3}{5}$ $6\frac{3}{4}$ $8\frac{4}{7}$ $4\frac{7}{8}$
$-2\frac{1}{6}$ $-2\frac{1}{10}$ $-2\frac{2}{4}$ $-3\frac{2}{14}$ $-2\frac{6}{8}$

D.

$8\frac{3}{4}$ $9\frac{3}{4}$ $6\frac{4}{9}$ $8\frac{1}{3}$ $4\frac{1}{6}$
$-2\frac{1}{6}$ $-3\frac{6}{12}$ $-2\frac{1}{3}$ $-3\frac{1}{4}$ $-2\frac{1}{12}$

 At Wet and Wild Water Park , the water at the end of Shake and Shiver water slide is 5 and 1/3 feet deep. The water at the end of Rolling Rapids water slide is 1 and 5/6 feet less deep than Shake and Shiver. How deep is the water at the end of Rolling Rapids?

A Great Way to Borrow

 When borrowing is necessary to subtract fractions, follow these steps.

$$5 \frac{2}{5} = 4 \frac{5}{5} + \frac{2}{5}$$
$$- 3 \frac{3}{5}$$

$$4 \frac{7}{5}$$
$$- 3 \frac{3}{5}$$

$$4 \frac{7}{5}$$
$$- 3 \frac{3}{5}$$
$$\frac{4}{5}$$

$$4 \frac{7}{5}$$
$$- 3 \frac{3}{5}$$
$$1 \frac{4}{5}$$

1. Borrow 1 from the whole number 5. Change 1 into the fraction 5/5.

2. Add 4 5/5 + 2/5.

3. Subtract the fractions.

4. Subtract the whole numbers. If necessary, reduce to lowest terms.

Add. Reduce to lowest terms. Then use the code below to answer the question.

Why is borrowing a good thing in math?

$$3 \frac{2}{6}$$
$$- 1 \frac{3}{6}$$

$$5 \frac{1}{4}$$
$$- 2 \frac{3}{4}$$

$$4 \frac{2}{5}$$
$$- 2 \frac{4}{5}$$

$$8 \frac{1}{3}$$
$$- 1 \frac{2}{3}$$

$$6 \frac{1}{8}$$
$$- 3 \frac{4}{8}$$

$$4 \frac{1}{7}$$
$$- 2 \frac{3}{7}$$

$$8 \frac{1}{4}$$
$$- 1 \frac{3}{4}$$

$$6 \frac{1}{3}$$
$$- 4 \frac{2}{3}$$

$$5 \frac{3}{12}$$
$$- 2 \frac{6}{12}$$

$$6 \frac{2}{4}$$
$$- 4 \frac{3}{4}$$

$$9 \frac{2}{8}$$
$$- 2 \frac{4}{8}$$

$$6 \frac{1}{8}$$
$$- 4 \frac{5}{8}$$

$$2 \frac{1}{9}$$
$$- 1 \frac{3}{9}$$

_____ !

at = 6 3/4	don't = 1 3/5
or = 2 5/8	owe = 6 2/3
of = 1 3/7	because = 1 5/6
the = 1 1/2	anything = 2 3/4
to = 6 1/2	have = 1 5/7
pay = 1 2/3	back = 1 3/4
end = 7/9	problem = 5 8/11
you = 2 1/2	

$$3 \frac{1}{7}$$
$$- 1 \frac{5}{7}$$

$$4 \frac{1}{6}$$
$$- 2 \frac{4}{6}$$

$$9 \frac{1}{11}$$
$$- 3 \frac{4}{11}$$

Name _____

Math Meteors

 To subtract fractions and mixed numbers from whole numbers, follow these steps.

$$5 = 4\frac{3}{3}$$
$$-\ 2\frac{1}{3}$$

$$4\frac{3}{3}$$
$$-\ 2\frac{1}{3}$$
$$\overline{\frac{2}{3}}$$

$$4\frac{3}{3}$$
$$-\ 2\frac{1}{3}$$
$$\overline{2\frac{2}{3}}$$

1. Change the whole number into a mixed number using the denominator of the fraction.

2. Subtract the fractions.

3. Subtract the whole numbers. If necessary, reduce to lowest terms.

Subtract. Reduce to lowest terms. Then use the code to learn about a famous meteorite.

E. 6
$-\ \frac{4}{8}$

I. 5
$-\ 2\frac{1}{2}$

T. 3
$-\ 1\frac{2}{5}$

A. 6
$-\ \frac{3}{7}$

L. 9
$-\ 6\frac{1}{4}$

W. 3
$-\ 1\frac{1}{3}$

E. 7
$-\ 2\frac{1}{5}$

L. 5
$-\ 1\frac{3}{5}$

T. 7
$-\ 2\frac{1}{3}$

C. 4
$-\ 2\frac{3}{5}$

N. 2
$-\ \frac{3}{7}$

G. 6
$-\ 3\frac{1}{5}$

S. 4
$-\ \frac{3}{7}$

M. 9
$-\ 3\frac{1}{6}$

J. 8
$-\ \frac{3}{7}$

The largest meteorite found in the United States is called the

___ ___ ___ ___ ___ ___ ___ ___ ___ **meteorite.**
$1\frac{2}{3}$ $2\frac{1}{2}$ $3\frac{2}{5}$ $2\frac{3}{4}$ $5\frac{4}{7}$ $5\frac{5}{6}$ $4\frac{4}{5}$ $1\frac{3}{5}$ $4\frac{2}{3}$ $5\frac{1}{2}$

Mighty Multiplication

To multiply a whole number and a fraction, follow these steps.

$$2 \times \frac{3}{4} \qquad \frac{2}{1} \times \frac{3}{4} \qquad \frac{2 \times 3}{1 \times 4} = \frac{6}{4} \qquad 1\frac{2}{4} = 1\frac{1}{2}$$

1. Change the whole number into a fraction.

2. Multiply the numerators and the denominators.

3. Change the improper fraction to a mixed number. Reduce to lowest terms.

$$7 \times \frac{1}{8}$$

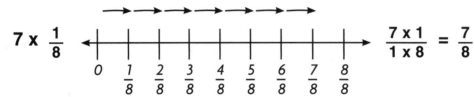

$$\frac{7 \times 1}{1 \times 8} = \frac{7}{8}$$

Multiply. Reduce to lowest terms.

A.
$3 \times \frac{2}{5} =$
$6 \times \frac{1}{3} =$
$7 \times \frac{1}{4} =$
$5 \times \frac{2}{3} =$

B.
$4 \times \frac{1}{2} =$
$4 \times \frac{1}{8} =$
$6 \times \frac{2}{3} =$
$6 \times \frac{4}{8} =$

C.
$5 \times \frac{3}{4} =$
$5 \times \frac{1}{6} =$
$8 \times \frac{1}{4} =$
$9 \times \frac{2}{3} =$

D.
$7 \times \frac{3}{5} =$
$9 \times \frac{1}{3} =$
$3 \times \frac{2}{4} =$
$4 \times \frac{5}{6} =$

E.
$7 \times \frac{2}{3} =$
$2 \times \frac{1}{3} =$
$9 \times \frac{1}{2} =$
$7 \times \frac{2}{8} =$

Muscular Marvin tried to lift 8 heavy boxes. They were too heavy. He then tried to lift 3/4 of the boxes. He succeeded! How many boxes did he lift?

It's Raining Multiplication

 To multiply fractions, multiply the numerators. Then multiply the denominators. Reduce to lowest terms.

$\dfrac{1}{2}$ of $\dfrac{1}{3}$ $\dfrac{1}{2}$ of $\dfrac{1}{3} = \dfrac{1}{6}$

$$\frac{1 \times 1}{2 \times 3} = \frac{1}{6}$$

Multiply. Reduce to lowest terms. Then write the ones digit in the denominator from each product in the raindrops in order on the lines below to learn a fact about rain.

A. $\dfrac{1}{3} \times \dfrac{2}{6} =$ $\dfrac{3}{5} \times \dfrac{2}{3} =$ $\dfrac{3}{4} \times \dfrac{1}{2} =$ $\dfrac{1}{4} \times \dfrac{1}{3} =$

B. $\dfrac{1}{5} \times \dfrac{1}{6} =$ $\dfrac{2}{4} \times \dfrac{1}{2} =$ $\dfrac{1}{4} \times \dfrac{2}{3} =$ $\dfrac{3}{4} \times \dfrac{1}{3} =$

C. $\dfrac{4}{8} \times \dfrac{1}{2} =$ $\dfrac{1}{8} \times \dfrac{1}{2} =$ $\dfrac{1}{5} \times \dfrac{1}{10} =$ $\dfrac{1}{3} \times \dfrac{1}{6} =$

D. $\dfrac{3}{5} \times \dfrac{1}{3} =$ $\dfrac{2}{6} \times \dfrac{1}{4} =$ $\dfrac{1}{3} \times \dfrac{1}{2} =$ $\dfrac{5}{8} \times \dfrac{2}{3} =$

E. $\dfrac{3}{7} \times \dfrac{3}{6} =$ $\dfrac{1}{5} \times \dfrac{1}{4} =$ $\dfrac{1}{2} \times \dfrac{1}{4} =$ $\dfrac{2}{3} \times \dfrac{3}{4} =$

F. $\dfrac{3}{5} \times \dfrac{1}{2} =$ $\dfrac{4}{6} \times \dfrac{2}{3} =$ $\dfrac{1}{2} \times \dfrac{1}{9} =$ $\dfrac{3}{4} \times \dfrac{2}{7} =$

Areas of Hawaii have over ____ ____ ____ **inches**
                                A   B   C

or ____ ____ ____ **centimeters of rain each year!**
      D   E   F

Crazy Word Combos

multiply fractions and mixed numbers, follow these steps.

$\frac{1}{3} \times 3\frac{1}{4}$ $3\frac{1}{4} = \frac{13}{4}$ $\frac{1}{3} \times \frac{13}{4} = \frac{13}{12}$ $\frac{13}{12} = 1\frac{1}{12}$

1. Change the mixed number into an improper fraction.
2. Multiply.
3. Change the improper fraction to a mixed number. Reduce to lowest terms.

Multiply. If the product can be reduced to a whole number or a fraction, unscramble the crazy word combo. Use the Word Bank below to help you. If the product is a mixed number, disregard.

$\frac{2}{3} \times 4\frac{1}{2} =$	$\frac{6}{7} \times 1\frac{1}{2} =$	$\frac{1}{5} \times 6\frac{1}{2} =$
d c n o a w h	h n f l u s e	a d x a l x

_____

$\frac{1}{5} \times 3\frac{1}{2} =$	$\frac{4}{5} \times 2\frac{1}{2} =$	$\frac{3}{5} \times 2\frac{1}{3} =$
m b r o o o w k	k b l o a a w d r	a q u r s t l

_____

$\frac{1}{2} \times 3\frac{1}{4} =$	$\frac{1}{6} \times 1\frac{1}{2} =$	$\frac{6}{7} \times 1\frac{1}{3} =$
m r a u s t u	y h l o f u e s	a l m n o o z e

_____

$\frac{3}{5} \times 3\frac{1}{3} =$	$\frac{3}{6} \times 1\frac{1}{3} =$	$\frac{1}{5} \times 1\frac{1}{3} =$
l t i o a e n	l c o a o r p	b w o c y o

_____

Word Bank

foxglove	cowhand	toenail	housefly
cowboy	carpool	boardwalk	bookworm

Division Stars

To divide a whole number by a fraction, follow these steps.

$$4 \div \frac{1}{3} = \qquad 4 = \frac{4}{1} \qquad \frac{1}{3} = \frac{3}{1} \qquad \frac{4 \times 3}{1 \times 1} = \frac{12}{1} \qquad \frac{12}{1} = 12$$

1. Change the whole number into a fraction.
2. Invert $\frac{1}{3}$.
3. Multiply.
4. Change the improper fraction to a mixed number. Reduce to lowest terms.

$$4 \div \frac{1}{3} = 12$$

    12 thirds.

Divide each of the 4 rectangles into thirds. Total thirds: 12

Divide. Then write the ones digit in each star in order on the lines below to learn about our star, the sun.

A. $7 \div \frac{1}{3} =$ $\qquad$ $7 \div \frac{1}{2} =$ $\qquad$ $4 \div \frac{1}{2} = \bigstar$ $\qquad$ $8 \div \frac{1}{4} =$ $\qquad$ $6 \div \frac{1}{2} =$

B. $3 \div \frac{1}{5} =$ $\qquad$ $3 \div \frac{1}{3} =$ $\qquad$ $9 \div \frac{1}{3} =$ $\qquad$ $2 \div \frac{1}{3} = \bigstar$ $\qquad$ $2 \div \frac{1}{4} =$

C. $5 \div \frac{1}{3} = \bigstar$ $\qquad$ $3 \div \frac{1}{2} =$ $\qquad$ $1 \div \frac{1}{2} =$ $\qquad$ $5 \div \frac{1}{6} = \bigstar$ $\qquad$ $4 \div \frac{1}{3} =$

D. $8 \div \frac{1}{2} =$ $\qquad$ $6 \div \frac{1}{3} =$ $\qquad$ $5 \div \frac{1}{2} = \bigstar$ $\qquad$ $5 \div \frac{1}{4} = \bigstar$ $\qquad$ $3 \div \frac{1}{4} =$

The diameter of the sun is ____ ____ ____, ____ ____ ____ **miles.**

The Great Divide

 To change a fraction to a decimal, follow these steps.

$$\frac{4}{10} \quad 10\overline{)4}$$

1. Divide the numerator by the denominator.

$$10\overline{)4}^{\,0}$$

2. Divide. Subtract. Add a decimal point and a zero. Divide.

$$10\overline{)4.0}^{\,0.4}$$

$$\begin{array}{r} 0.4 \\ 10\overline{)4.0} \\ -4\,0 \\ \hline 0 \end{array}$$

3. Subtract.

$$\frac{4}{10} = 0.4$$

Change each fraction to a decimal.

A. $\frac{1}{5} =$ $\frac{3}{6} =$ $\frac{4}{5} =$ $\frac{2}{5} =$

B. $\frac{3}{4} =$ $\frac{3}{8} =$ $\frac{6}{10} =$ $\frac{7}{8} =$

C. $\frac{5}{25} =$ $\frac{1}{4} =$ $\frac{3}{10} =$ $\frac{5}{20} =$

D. $\frac{3}{25} =$ $\frac{4}{8} =$ $\frac{7}{20} =$ $\frac{9}{25} =$

E. $\frac{7}{10} =$ $\frac{5}{8} =$ $\frac{9}{10} =$ $\frac{3}{5} =$

 The Sorenson family ordered a large deluxe pizza. Jack ate 1/8 of the pizza. Lee ate 3/8 of the pizza. Tyler ate 4/8 of the pizza. Write the decimal for the fraction each person ate. Did they eat the whole pizza?

Triangular Patterns

 To change a decimal to a fraction, use the greatest common factor to reduce to lowest terms.

$$0.8 = \frac{8 \div 2}{10 \div 2} = \frac{4}{5} \qquad 0.40 = \frac{40 \div 20}{100 \div 20} = \frac{2}{5} \qquad 0.250 = \frac{250 \div 250}{1,000 \div 250} = \frac{1}{4}$$

Using a ruler, draw a line to match each decimal with its fraction.

$\frac{34}{100}$

0.5

0.25

$\frac{247}{1,000}$

0.37

$\frac{1}{100}$

0.3

$\frac{3}{10}$

0.7

$\frac{4}{5}$

0.547

$\frac{547}{1,000}$

0.75

$\frac{3}{4}$

0.9

$\frac{9}{10}$

0.34

0.01

$\frac{37}{100}$

0.8

$\frac{1}{4}$

$\frac{1}{2}$

0.247 $\frac{7}{10}$

 See how many triangles you can find in the diagram.

What's the Word?

From the right of the decimal point, decimals are read as tenths, hundredths, and thousandths.

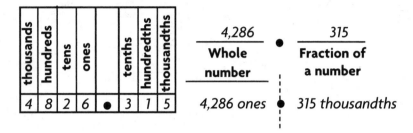

Draw a line from each decimal to its word name.

five and three thousandths	four and one hundredth	three hundred forty-two and one tenth	three and twelve hundredths

thirteen and four hundredths	**3.12**	**6.1**	**56.4**	three hundred two thousandths

5.003

	5.31	**4.01**	**13.04**	
sixty-one and four hundredths			**8.3**	fifty-six and four tenths

0.302

eight and forty-one thousands	**61.04**			five and thirty-one hundredths
	5.214	**1.002**	**3.22**	

six and one tenth	**8.041**	**981.42**	**342.1**	eight and three tenths

one and two thousandths	three and twenty-two hundredths	five and two hundred fourteen thousandths	nine hundred eighty-one and forty-two hundredths

Name _____

Polly Want a Cracker?

 The first digit to the right of the decimal point is the **tenths** *place.*

Write each decimal. Match each decimal diagram with a word in the Decimal Key below to find out what Polly wants.

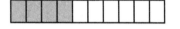   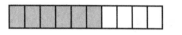   (image: 0.1 diagram)

_____   _____   _____

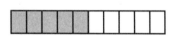      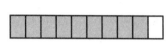

_____   _____   _____

      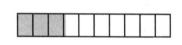

_____   _____   _____

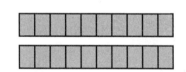   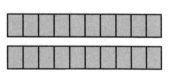   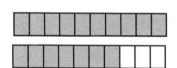

_____

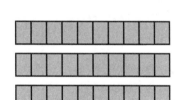   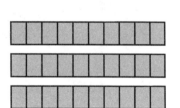   

_____

Decimal Key

only = 0.6	tenth = 0.1	cracker = 0.8	that = 0.7	one = 0.5	I = 0.4
your = 5.7	in = 0.3	hand! = 8.3	want = 0.2	of: 0.9	

 Sarah's pet parrot Chatter nibbled 2.3 crackers. On another sheet of paper, draw a diagram to show how many crackers Chatter nibbled.

Let's Go Digital!

The second digit to the right of the decimal is the **hundredths** place.

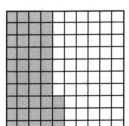

There are 43 hundredths (0.43) shaded in this diagram. That is 43 of the one hundred squares available.

Decimal: 0.43

Fraction: $\frac{43}{100}$

ones		tenths	hundredths
0	•	4	3

It is read forty-three hundredths.

Write the decimal for each number word in the Decimal Digital Boxes.

Decimal Digital Box

A. three and fifty-four hundredths

B. fifty-six and seventy-two hundredths

C. ninety-eight hundredths

D. twenty-four and two hundredths

E. three hundred four and three hundredths

F. seventy-five and thirteen hundredths

G. eight hundred forty-three and six hundredths

H. eighty-nine and twenty-two hundredths

I. one hundred thirty-one and seventy-one hundredths

J. sixty-nine hundredths

A. _____

B. _____

C. _____

D. _____

E. _____

F. _____

G. _____

H. _____

I. _____

J. _____

Decimal Digital Box

K. fifty-two and thirty-two hundredths

L. four hundred and fifty-seven hundredths

M. twenty-seven and four hundredths

N. forty-eight and three hundredths

O. fourteen and sixty-two hundredths

P. seven hundred eighty-six and two hundredths

Q. four hundred forty-five and sixty-four hundredths

R. six hundred twenty-five and fifty-four hundredths

S. nine hundred twenty-eight and twenty-four hundredths

T. four and nine tenths

K. _____

L. _____

M. _____

N. _____

O. _____

P. _____

Q. _____

R. _____

S. _____

T. _____

Put on Your Thinking Cap

*The third digit to the right of the decimal is the **thousandths** place.*

thousands	hundreds	tens	ones		tenths	hundredths	thousandths
3	2	3	6	●	0	0	4

ones		tenths	hundredths	thousandths
1	●	3	2	4

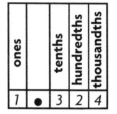

These decimals are read as follows: three thousand two hundred thirty-six and four thousandths   one and three hundred twenty-four thousandths

Use the clues to find each missing number.

A. This number has a 9 in the thousandths place and a 1 in the ones place. The total sum of the digits is 17. There are no 3s or 5s and all the digits are greater than 0. The lesser digit is in the tenths place.

_____ . _____ _____ _____

C. Get ready for a tough one! All the digits are different odd numbers between 0 and 10. The number with the greatest value is in the thousands place. The number with the least value is in the tenths place. The remaining numbers are in numerical order beginning in the hundreds place.

_____ , _____ _____ _____ . _____

B. Think hard! There is a 3 in the tens place, a 6 in the thousandths place, and nothing in between except for 2 ones.

_____ _____ . _____ _____ _____

D. Are you up for a challenge? This decimal has a 7 to the left of the decimal point. The sum of the three digits to the right of the decimal point is 15. The greatest of these three digits is one more than 7 and is in the hundredths place. The digit in the tenths place is less than the digit in the thousandths place and is greater than 2.

_____ . _____ _____ _____

E. A real challenge! The two digits to the left of the decimal point are different numbers and their sum is 10. They do not include a 1, 3, or 8. The number with the least value is in the tens place. To the right of the decimal point, the sum of the three digits also totals 10. Two of the digits are the same. The digit in the thousandths place is different than the digits in the tenths and hundredths places and is the same as the digit in the tens place.

_____ _____ . _____ _____ _____

💡 **Read each of the numbers above to a friend.**

Cross-Decimal Fun

Write the number word for each decimal. Use hyphens when necessary.

Across

1. 0.6
3. 0.08
4. 0.054
5. 0.5
6. 0.3

7. 0.02
8. 0.09
10. 0.05
11. 0.32
12. 0.026

Down

1. 0.007
2. 0.06

4. 0.4
9. 0.2

A Weighty Decision

A number line can be used to compare decimals.

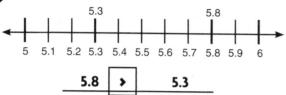

| 5.8 | > | 5.3 |

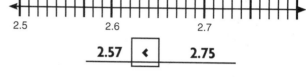

| 2.57 | < | 2.75 |

Eight tenths (5.8) is greater than three tenths (5.3).
Moving to the right on a number line increases the value of a decimal.

Fifty-seven hundredths (2.57) is less than seventy-five hundredths (2.75).
Moving to the left on a number line decreases the value of a decimal.

Write >, <, or = to compare the decimals. Then look at the decimal where the sign is pointing to. Write the letter or number above the decimal in order on the lines below to answer the question. If there is an = sign, write both letters in order.

N 3.4 ☐ Q 3.5	S 6.4 ☐ E 4.6	I 5.7 ☐ U 5.8	T 0.4 ☐ S 0.6
N 0.8 ☐ H 0.1	E 0.1 ☐ R 0.10	J 0.5 ☐ T 0.05	H 6.41 ☐ E 6.41
Y 7.4 ☐ R 7.40	M 0.41 ☐ E 0.4	U 3.2 ☐ B 0.32	B 9.02 ☐ O 0.92
X 0.7 ☐ T 0.07	H 8.4 ☐ Q 78.4	E 6.1 ☐ A 6.18	Q 0.6 ☐ N 0.8
V 5.1 ☐ U 0.05	A 2.9 ☐ M 9.2	L 0.1 ☐ R 1.01	W 8.4 ☐ L 4.8
Y 0.3 ☐ A 3.03	7 6.8 ☐ 3 6.40	5 2.41 ☐ 2 24.1	6 9.3 ☐ 7 3.4
5 2.48 ☐ 4 24.8			

Which is greater in weight? 3.575 pounds of feathers, or 3.575 pounds of cotton balls?

__ __ __ __ __ __ __ ! __ __ __ __ __ __ __ __ , __ __

__ __ __ __ __ __ __ __ __ __ . __ __ __ **pounds!**

That's an Order!

 To put decimals in order from least to greatest, compare digits in the same places.

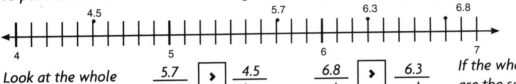

Look at the whole number. If they are different, compare.

$\dfrac{5.7}{\uparrow}$ ▸ $\dfrac{4.5}{\uparrow}$ $\dfrac{6.8}{\uparrow}$ ▸ $\dfrac{6.3}{\uparrow}$

If the whole numbers are the same, look at the decimals. Compare.

Order each set of decimals from least to greatest. Then write the letters in the same order to spell a math term in the last column.

A.	**H** 4.9	**A** 4.4	**T** 4.8	**M** 4.2	4.2	4.4	4.8	4.9	MATH
B.	**D** 7.7	**O** 7.3	**E** 7.9	**M** 7.0	—	—	—	—	_____
C.	**D** 0.8	**I** 0.5	**R** 0.3	**G** 0.2	—	—	—	—	_____
D.	**R** 3.6	**A** 8.4	**E** 5.7	**A** 1.9	—	—	—	—	_____
E.	**B** 2.89	**E** 2.98	**U** 2.47	**C** 2.16	—	—	—	—	_____
F.	**E** 8.42	**F** 0.59	**C** 6.48	**A** 3.93	—	—	—	—	_____
G.	**E** 4.09	**A** 6.409	**M** 0.409	**N** 6.904	—	—	—	—	_____
H.	**N** 4.06	**I** 3.92	**L** 0.92	**E** 6.9	—	—	—	—	_____
I.	**H** 9.08	**N** 4.84	**C** 5.45	**I** 1.8	—	—	—	—	_____
J.	**P** 1.842	**I** 1.824	**F** 1.248	**L** 1.482	—	—	—	—	_____
K.	**M** 9.05	**E** 5.09	**T** 0.59	**R** 9.005	—	—	—	—	_____

On another sheet of paper, make your own decimal and letter code to spell decimal. Use the same whole number for each decimal. Have a friend put the decimals and the letters in order.

The Big Roundup (or Down!)

When rounding, if the number is 5 or more, round up. If the number is 4 or less, round down.

3.<u>6</u> = 4
8.<u>4</u> = 8

6.3<u>4</u> = 6.3
9.6<u>6</u> = 9.7

When rounding to the nearest whole number, look at the tenths digit.

When rounding to the nearest tenth, look at the hundredths digit.

Write each decimal and the rounded number in the correct box.

A. Round to nearest whole number.

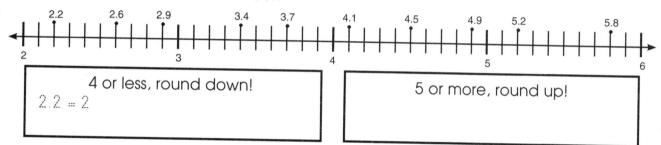

4 or less, round down!	5 or more, round up!
2.2 = 2	

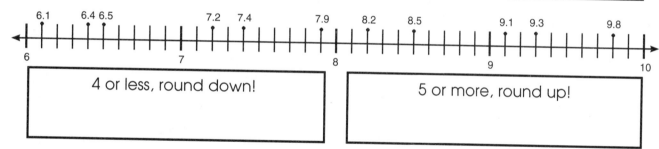

4 or less, round down!	5 or more, round up!

B. Round to nearest tenth.

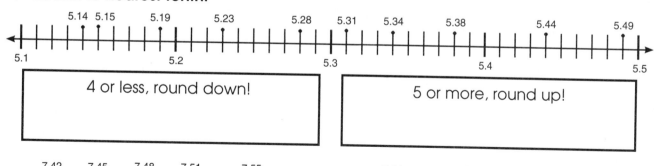

4 or less, round down!	5 or more, round up!

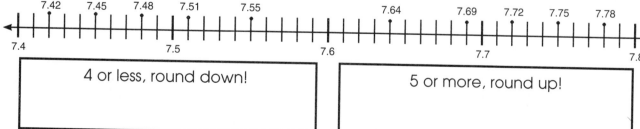

4 or less, round down!	5 or more, round up!

Let's Get Rolling!

Round the decimals on each set of rocks to the nearest hundredths place. Then write the rounded decimals in order from least to greatest.

A.

0.192 _____

0.618 _____

0.542 _____

0.849 _____

0.651 _____

0.658 _____

0.329 _____

0.912 _____

0.689 _____

0.745 _____

_____ _____ _____ _____ _____

_____ _____ _____ _____ _____

B.

6.416 _____

5.914 _____

4.255 _____

3.692 _____

5.346 _____

4.182 _____

3.145 _____

6.545 _____

7.312 _____

9.425 _____

_____ _____ _____ _____ _____

_____ _____ _____ _____ _____

 On another sheet of paper, write three decimals that could be rounded to 5.7 and three decimals that could be rounded to 2.64.

Name _____

Pile Them Up!

 When adding decimals, follow these steps.

36.46	¹ ¹ 36.46	¹ ¹ 36.46	¹ 36.46
+ 13.84	+ 13.84	+ 13.84	+ 13.84
∙ 0	.30	0.30	50.30

1. Line up the decimal points. Add the hundredths. Regroup.

2. Add the tenths. Regroup.

3. Add the ones. Regroup.

4. Add the tens.

Choose two addends from the decimal pile to make each sum.

A.

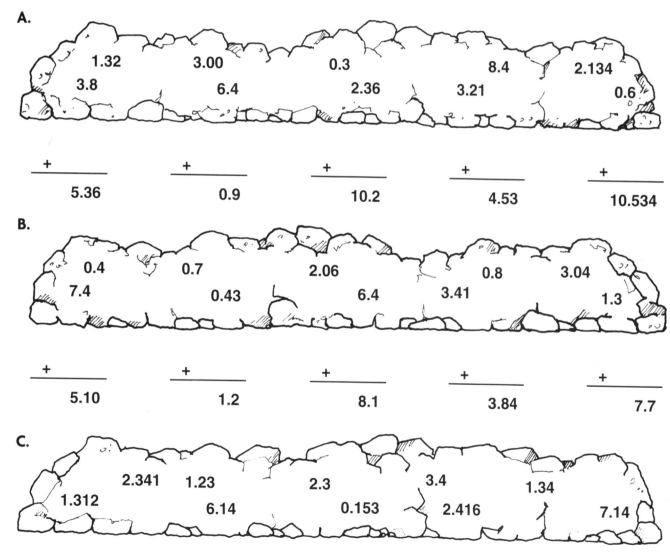

1.32   3.00   0.3   8.4   2.134

3.8   6.4   2.36   3.21   0.6

+	+	+	+	+
5.36	0.9	10.2	4.53	10.534

B.

0.4   0.7   2.06   0.8   3.04

7.4   0.43   6.4   3.41   1.3

+	+	+	+	+
5.10	1.2	8.1	3.84	7.7

C.

2.341   1.23   2.3   3.4   1.34

1.312   6.14   0.153   2.416   7.14

+	+	+	+	+
5.7	7.37	2.494	8.48	3.728

Geometric Code Crackers

Use the Shape Bank to write each problem. Add.

Shape Bank

△	=	3.214
□	=	21.04
▱	=	1.048
○	=	34.218
◿	=	7.06
⬡	=	23.142
⬠	=	0.343
▭	=	6.2
◇	=	0.246
⏢	=	1.003
⬠	=	2.14
◈◈	=	13.102
◬	=	0.243
⬓	=	8.141
⬭	=	0.203
☆	=	26.31

A.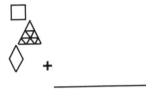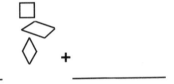

B.

C.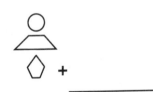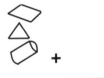

D.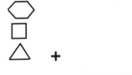

E.

F.

Name _____

Let's Get Going!

 To subtract decimals, follow these steps.

$$\begin{array}{r} \cancel{8}.23 \\ -\ 1.345 \\ \hline . \end{array}$$

1. Line up the decimal points. Place the decimal in the answer.

$$\begin{array}{r} 8.2\overset{2}{\cancel{3}}\overset{1}{0} \\ -\ 1.345 \\ \hline .\ 5 \end{array}$$

2. Add a zero to make the same number of digits. Borrow. Regroup. Subtract the thousandths.

$$\begin{array}{r} 8.\overset{1}{\cancel{2}}\overset{12}{3}\overset{1}{0} \\ -\ 1.345 \\ \hline .\ 85 \end{array}$$

3. Borrow. Regroup. Subtract the hundredths.

$$\begin{array}{r} \overset{7}{\cancel{8}}.\overset{11}{\cancel{2}}\overset{12}{3}\overset{1}{0} \\ -\ 1.345 \\ \hline .885 \end{array}$$

4. Borrow. Regroup. Subtract the tenths.

$$\begin{array}{r} \overset{7}{\cancel{8}}.\overset{11}{\cancel{2}}\overset{12}{3}\overset{1}{0} \\ -\ 1.345 \\ \hline 6.885 \end{array}$$

5. Subtract the ones.

Subtract.

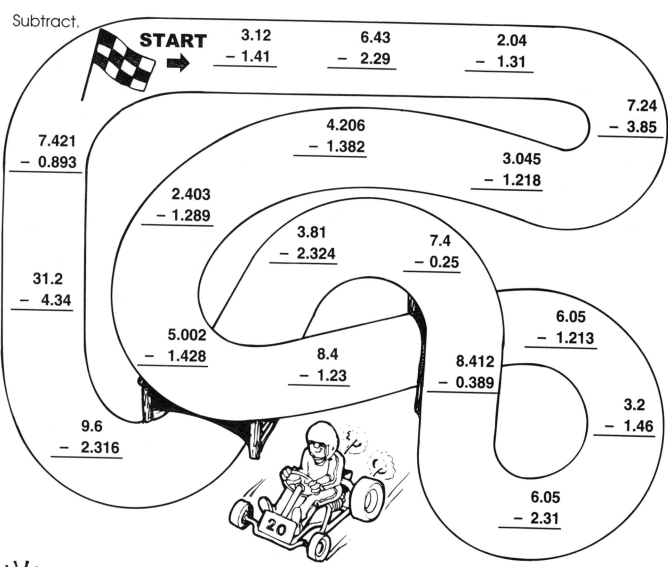

START →

3.12	
− 1.41	

| 6.43 |
| − 2.29 |

| 2.04 |
| − 1.31 |

| 7.24 |
| − 3.85 |

| 7.421 |
| − 0.893 |

| 4.206 |
| − 1.382 |

| 3.045 |
| − 1.218 |

| 2.403 |
| − 1.289 |

| 3.81 |
| − 2.324 |

| 7.4 |
| − 0.25 |

| 31.2 |
| − 4.34 |

| 5.002 |
| − 1.428 |

| 8.4 |
| − 1.23 |

| 8.412 |
| − 0.389 |

| 6.05 |
| − 1.213 |

| 3.2 |
| − 1.46 |

| 9.6 |
| − 2.316 |

| 6.05 |
| − 2.31 |

 Drew completed two laps around the go-cart track. It took him 4.26 minutes to complete the first lap and 3.47 minutes to complete the second lap. How much faster did he complete the first lap?

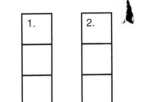

Cross-Decimal Subtraction

 To subtract a decimal from a whole number, add a zero for each decimal place. Subtract.

$$\begin{array}{r} 3 \\ -\ 0.246 \end{array} \qquad \begin{array}{r} {}^{2\ 9\ 9}\!\!\!\!\!\!\!\!3.000 \\ -\ 0.246 \\ \hline 2.754 \end{array}$$

Subtract. Decimal points count as a space.

Across:

4.
$$\begin{array}{r} 8 \\ -\ 5.002 \end{array}$$

5.
$$\begin{array}{r} 2 \\ -\ 0.982 \end{array}$$

6.
$$\begin{array}{r} 4 \\ -\ 2.467 \end{array}$$

7.
$$\begin{array}{r} 3 \\ -\ 2.403 \end{array}$$

8.
$$\begin{array}{r} 5 \\ -\ 2.48 \end{array}$$

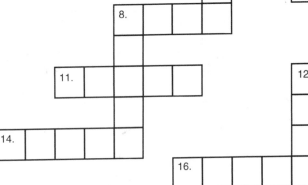

Down:

9.
$$\begin{array}{r} 13 \\ -\ 2.89 \end{array}$$

11.
$$\begin{array}{r} 9 \\ -\ 3.546 \end{array}$$

1.
$$\begin{array}{r} 4 \\ -\ 2.006 \end{array}$$

2.
$$\begin{array}{r} 6 \\ -\ 3.419 \end{array}$$

3.
$$\begin{array}{r} 5 \\ -\ 3.891 \end{array}$$

4.
$$\begin{array}{r} 5 \\ -\ 2.642 \end{array}$$

14.
$$\begin{array}{r} 7 \\ -\ 3.002 \end{array}$$

15.
$$\begin{array}{r} 12 \\ -\ 2.412 \end{array}$$

6.
$$\begin{array}{r} 2 \\ -\ 0.48 \end{array}$$

7.
$$\begin{array}{r} 3 \\ -\ 2.19 \end{array}$$

8.
$$\begin{array}{r} 6 \\ -\ 3.592 \end{array}$$

10.
$$\begin{array}{r} 3 \\ -\ 2.146 \end{array}$$

16.
$$\begin{array}{r} 7 \\ -\ 2.455 \end{array}$$

17.
$$\begin{array}{r} 6 \\ -\ 0.324 \end{array}$$

12.
$$\begin{array}{r} 6 \\ -\ 3.145 \end{array}$$

13.
$$\begin{array}{r} 10 \\ -\ 5.033 \end{array}$$

Name _____

A Smart Butterfly

When multiplying with decimals, place the decimal point in the product, counting from right to left, the same number of places as the sum of the decimal places in the factors.

$6.95
x   3
The decimal point is 2 places, counting from right to left, in the top factor. There is no decimal point in the bottom factor. 2 + 0 = 2

$6.95
x   3
$20.85
Place the decimal point 2 places, counting from right to left, in the product.

Multiply. Then use the code to answer the riddle below.

I.	E.	A.	T.	W.	O.
2.8 x 3	26.5 x 4	32.8 x 7	20.41 x 5	0.24 x 9	0.04 x 8

H.	S.	I.	T.	I.	M.
3.06 x 6	300.1 x 8	24.81 x 6	24.6 x 5	41.5 x 3	0.416 x 5

T.	M.	C.	N.	A.	A.
45.6 x 8	48.5 x 3	4.53 x 3	3.08 x 4	3.49 x 7	6.94 x 9

Why did the butterfly learn decimals?

___ ___   ___ ___ ___   ___
124.5 123.0   2.16 62.46 240.08   229.6

___ ___ ___ ___ — ___ ___ ___ ___ ___ ___ ___ ___ ___ .
2.080 0.32 102.5 18.36   106.0 145.5 24.43 364.8 148.86 13.59 8.4 132.88 12.32

Name _____

Skywriting, Decimal Style

 To multiply decimals, follow these steps.

$$\begin{array}{r} \overset{1}{4.6} \\ \times\ 3.2 \\ \hline 92 \\ 0 \end{array}$$

1. Multiply by the tenth digit. Add a zero.

$$\begin{array}{r} \overset{1}{4.6} \\ \times\ 3.2 \\ \hline 92 \\ 1380 \end{array}$$

2. Multiply by the ones digit.

$$\begin{array}{r} \overset{1}{4.6} \\ \times\ 3.2 \\ \hline \overset{1}{92} \\ 1380 \\ \hline 1472 \end{array}$$

3. Add.

$$\begin{array}{r} 4.6 \\ \times\ 3.2 \\ \hline 92 \\ 1380 \\ \hline 14.72 \end{array}$$

4. Starting from right to left in each factor, count the number of spaces to the decimal point. Place the decimal point in the product.

To discover what the sky writer wrote, shade in each cloud with a product greater than 1.

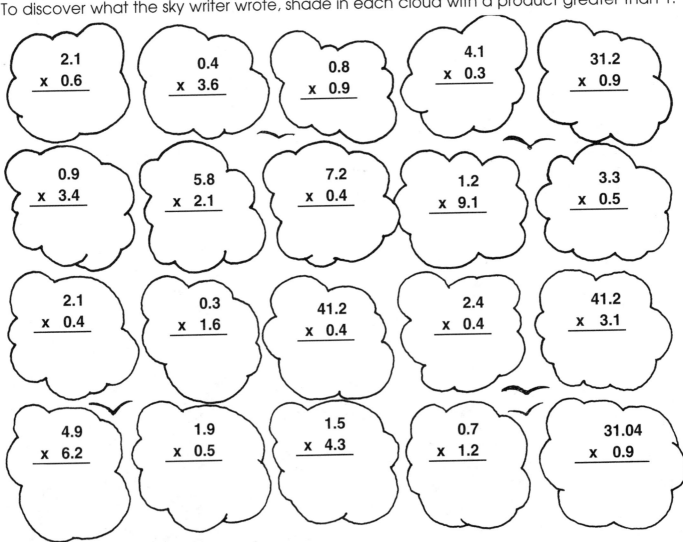

$$\begin{array}{r} 2.1 \\ \times\ 0.6 \end{array}$$

$$\begin{array}{r} 0.4 \\ \times\ 3.6 \end{array}$$

$$\begin{array}{r} 0.8 \\ \times\ 0.9 \end{array}$$

$$\begin{array}{r} 4.1 \\ \times\ 0.3 \end{array}$$

$$\begin{array}{r} 31.2 \\ \times\ 0.9 \end{array}$$

$$\begin{array}{r} 0.9 \\ \times\ 3.4 \end{array}$$

$$\begin{array}{r} 5.8 \\ \times\ 2.1 \end{array}$$

$$\begin{array}{r} 7.2 \\ \times\ 0.4 \end{array}$$

$$\begin{array}{r} 1.2 \\ \times\ 9.1 \end{array}$$

$$\begin{array}{r} 3.3 \\ \times\ 0.5 \end{array}$$

$$\begin{array}{r} 2.1 \\ \times\ 0.4 \end{array}$$

$$\begin{array}{r} 0.3 \\ \times\ 1.6 \end{array}$$

$$\begin{array}{r} 41.2 \\ \times\ 0.4 \end{array}$$

$$\begin{array}{r} 2.4 \\ \times\ 0.4 \end{array}$$

$$\begin{array}{r} 41.2 \\ \times\ 3.1 \end{array}$$

$$\begin{array}{r} 4.9 \\ \times\ 6.2 \end{array}$$

$$\begin{array}{r} 1.9 \\ \times\ 0.5 \end{array}$$

$$\begin{array}{r} 1.5 \\ \times\ 4.3 \end{array}$$

$$\begin{array}{r} 0.7 \\ \times\ 1.2 \end{array}$$

$$\begin{array}{r} 31.04 \\ \times\ 0.9 \end{array}$$

 The sky writer made 9.6 loops in his plane. It took him 1.8 minutes to make each loop. How long did it take him to make all the loops?

Zero, You're Such a Hero!

Zero is such an important number when multiplying decimals. Remember, always place a zero to the left of a decimal point when there are no whole numbers present.

0.004	0.004	0.004	0.004 (3 places)
x 0.6	x 0.6	x 0.6	x 0.6 (1 place)
0024	0024	0024	0024
0	00000	00000	00000
		00024	0.0024

1. Multiply the tenths digit. Add a zero under the first digit to the right.

2. Multiply the ones digit.

3. Add.

4. Place the decimal point in the product.

A million has 6 zeros. To find out how many zeros a septillion has, count the number of zeros to the right of the decimal point in each of the problems.

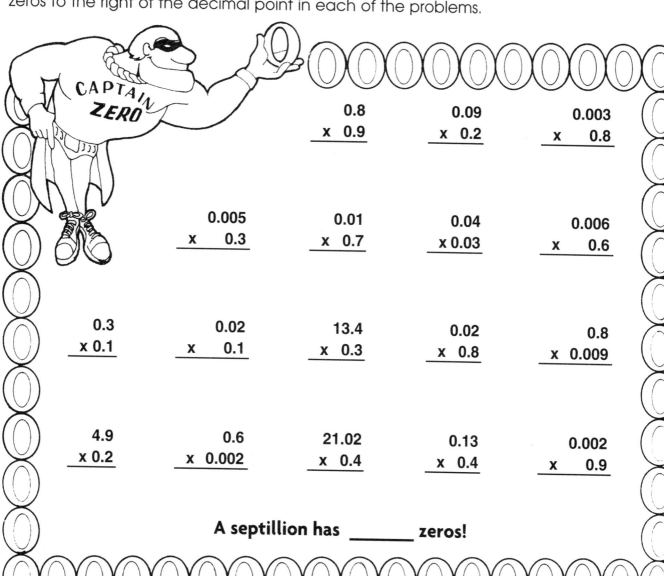

0.8	0.09	0.003
x 0.9	x 0.2	x 0.8

0.005	0.01	0.04	0.006
x 0.3	x 0.7	x 0.03	x 0.6

0.3	0.02	13.4	0.02	0.8
x 0.1	x 0.1	x 0.3	x 0.8	x 0.009

4.9	0.6	21.02	0.13	0.002
x 0.2	x 0.002	x 0.4	x 0.4	x 0.9

A septillion has _____ zeros!

Name _____

Keep on Climbing

 To divide decimals by a whole number, follow these steps.

$$\begin{array}{r} 2 \\ 3\overline{)7.44} \\ -6 \\ \hline 1 \end{array}$$

$$\begin{array}{r} 2.4 \\ 3\overline{)7.44} \\ -6 \\ \hline 14 \\ -12 \\ \hline 2 \end{array}$$

$$\begin{array}{r} 2.48 \\ 3\overline{)7.44} \\ -6 \\ \hline 14 \\ -12 \\ \hline 24 \\ -24 \\ \hline 0 \end{array}$$

If the quotient is less than one, there must be a zero to the left of the decimal point.

$$0.58 < 1$$

$$\begin{array}{r} 0.58 \\ 2\overline{)1.16} \\ -10 \\ \hline 16 \\ -16 \\ \hline 0 \end{array}$$

1. Divide the ones.

2. Place the decimal point in the quotient. Divide the tenths.

3. Divide the hundredths.

Divide. Then use the code to fill in the blanks below to complete the fact about two famous mountain climbers.

U.
$4\overline{)8.64}$

L.
$2\overline{)72.8}$

S.
$6\overline{)9.36}$

Y.
$5\overline{)32.35}$

H.
$5\overline{)23.5}$

R.
$9\overline{)5.22}$

E.
$3\overline{)267.3}$

M.
$2\overline{)13.56}$

D.
$3\overline{)2.67}$

A.
$2\overline{)1.18}$

N.
$3\overline{)110.4}$

I.
$4\overline{)107.2}$

The first men to climb the top of Mount Everest were Tenzing Norgay and

___ ___ ___   ___ ___ ___ ___ ___ ___
1.56 26.8 0.58   89.1 0.89 6.78 2.16 36.8 0.89

___ ___ ___ ___ ___ ___ ___ .
4.7 26.8 36.4 36.4 0.59 0.58 6.47

Name _____

Ride the Wave of Decimal Division

Sometimes zeros are needed in the quotient. When dividing decimals by a whole number, follow these steps.

$$\begin{array}{r} 2 \\ 27\overline{)55.08} \\ -54 \\ \hline 1 \end{array}$$

1. Divide the whole number.

$$\begin{array}{r} 2. \\ 27\overline{)55.08} \\ -54 \\ \hline 1 \end{array}$$

2. Place the decimal point in the quotient.

$$\begin{array}{r} 2.0 \\ 27\overline{)55.08} \\ -54 \\ \hline 10 \ (< 27) \end{array}$$

3. Bring down the 0. Since it is still < 27, place a zero in the quotient.

$$\begin{array}{r} 2.04 \\ 27\overline{)55.08} \\ -54 \\ \hline 108 \\ -108 \\ \hline 0 \end{array}$$

4. Bring down the 8. Divide into 108.

Divide. Then write the letter for each quotient from least to greatest on the lines below to learn where the 1958 megatsunami occurred.

B. $62\overline{)126.48}$

L. $13\overline{)3.12}$

Y. $41\overline{)102.50}$

A. $17\overline{)51.85}$

A. $13\overline{)62.4}$

K. $14\overline{)84.14}$

I. $51\overline{)18.36}$

S. $17\overline{)86.02}$

A. $39\overline{)81.12}$

U. $16\overline{)11.04}$

T. $32\overline{)18.56}$

L. $21\overline{)64.89}$

A. $44\overline{)46.64}$

Y. $51\overline{)53.856}$

A. $31\overline{)188.17}$

The wave occurred in ____ ____ ____ ____ ____

____ ____ ____ in ____ ____ ____ ____ ____ ____ . It reached 1,720 feet.

Copyright © Scholastic Inc.

Name _____

**Adding zeros to
the dividend**

Lots of Zeros

 When dividing decimals, add zeros to the dividend to continue dividing.

$$\begin{array}{r} 0 \\ 5 \overline{)4} \end{array} \qquad \begin{array}{r} 0. \\ 5 \overline{)4} \end{array} \qquad \begin{array}{r} 0. \\ 5 \overline{)40} \end{array} \qquad \begin{array}{r} 0.8 \\ 5 \overline{)40} \\ -40 \\ \hline 0 \end{array}$$

1. Does 5 divide into 4? No. Place a zero in the quotient.
2. Place the decimal point in the quotient.
3. Add a zero to the dividend.
4. Divide.

Divide.

A. $5\overline{)16}$ $\quad$ $4\overline{)23.1}$ $\quad$ $8\overline{)5.3}$ $\quad$ $8\overline{)27}$ $\quad$ $5\overline{)2.8}$

B. $5\overline{)4.1}$ $\quad$ $8\overline{)14}$ $\quad$ $4\overline{)7}$ $\quad$ $8\overline{)27}$ $\quad$ $4\overline{)8.9}$

C. $4\overline{)31}$ $\quad$ $2\overline{)6.1}$ $\quad$ $5\overline{)8}$ $\quad$ $8\overline{)23}$ $\quad$ $5\overline{)6.8}$

D. $5\overline{)5.6}$ $\quad$ $5\overline{)7.4}$ $\quad$ $4\overline{)3}$ $\quad$ $8\overline{)45}$ $\quad$ $8\overline{)2.1}$

 Will completed 4 division problems in 3 minutes. How long did it take him to solve each problem?

Copyright © Scholastic Inc.

46 **Scholastic Success With Fractions & Decimals**

Page 4
2/4, 1/3, 1/2; 6/12, 4/8, 5/9, 3/8; 1/4, 5/12, 2/6

Page 5
A. 3, 2, 2; B. 2, 2, 9; C. 15, 25, 6; D. 24, 4, 10; E. 3, 5, 3; 10 shells at school, 15 shells at her house

Page 6
A. 1/4 = 2/8, 1/3 = 3/9, 2/3 = 12/18, 1/2 = 6/12; B. 6, 6, 6, 6; C. 30, 10, 12, 21; D. 16, 27, 15, 70

Page 7

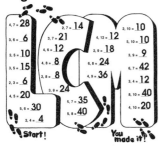

Page 8
A. Factors of 5: 1, 5; Factors of 15: 1, 3, 5, 15; 5; B. Factors of 6: 1, 2, 3, 6; Factors of 18: 1, 2, 3, 6, 9, 18; 6; C. Factors of 3: 1, 3; Factors of 21: 1, 3, 7, 21; 3; D. Factors of 7: 1, 7; Factors of 28: 1, 2, 4, 7, 14, 28; 7; E. ÷ 2 = 2/5, ÷ 6 = 1/2, ÷ 3 = 1/4; F. ÷ 4 = 1/5, ÷ 3 = 1/7; ÷ 5 = 1/3; G. ÷ 7 = 1/3, ÷ 3 = 1/8, ÷ 7 = 1/4

Page 9

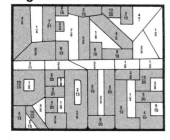

4/8 = 1/2, 7/21 = 1/3, 2/10 = 1/5, 10/20 = 1/2, 3/15 = 1/5; 6/8 = 3/4, 6/12 = 1/2, 3/6 = 1/2, 6/10 = 3/5, 4/6 = 2/3, 9/18 = 1/2; 10/15 = 2/3, 2/20 = 1/10, 3/21 =

1/7, 5/10 = 1/2, 5/20 = 1/4, 2/6 = 1/3, 15/20 = 3/4; 4/12 = 1/3, 10/12 = 5/6, 4/20 = 1/5, 3/9 = 1/3, 2/8 = 1/4, 8/20 = 2/5, 8/12 = 2/3, 5/30 = 1/6, 4/10 = 2/5

Page 10
A. <, =, >, <; B. >, >, >, =; C. >, >, >, >; They both ate the same amount.

Page 11
A. 2 4/7, B. 4, C. 3 4/5, E. 3 3/4, H. 2 5/7, I. 4 2/3, K. 4 1/4, R. 7 2/4, S. 2, T. 1 3/4, U. 3 2/6, W. 2 1/5
BECAUSE IT SAW THE TREE BARK!

Page 12

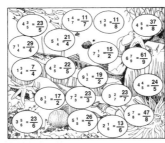

51/4 silver coins

Page 13
Kids will vote yea and horses neigh! (nay) They'd rather be munching and crunching on oats and hay!

Page 14
A. 5/8, O; 3/4, X; 2/3, O; 3/8, X; 3/10, X; 3/6 = 1/2, X; 6/10 = 3/5, O; 4/15, O; 4/9, X; B. 7/8, O; 3/12 = 1/4, O; 5/12, X; 6/6 = 1, O; 7/12, O; 5/6, X; 3/14, X; 7/16, X; 7/9, O

Page 15
O. 5/6; W. 7/12; E. 7/10; G. 17/21; S. 1 7/15; A. 2/3; L. 11/28; O. 11/15; I. 1 11/20; N. 13/18; R. 17/20; D. 1 1/6; H. 1 9/40; ! 8/15; U. 37/56; N. 3/4; Y. 19/28; HE WAS ALWAYS HORSING AROUND!

Page 16
A. 4 5/8, 7 1/6, 5 1/4; B. 3 1/2, 3 2/3, 3 5/6; C. 7 5/6, 5 1/8, 5 2/3, 6 2/3; D. 6 2/3, 3 7/9, 9 1/6, 5 1/8; E. 3 17/20, 4 5/8, 10 1/5, 4 7/10; 2 3/4 + 3 4/8 = 6 1/4 hours

Page 17
A. 1/14; B. 2/15, C. 1/4, D. 7/12; E. 1/14, F. 8/25, G. 1/4; H. 1/10; I. 2/9; J. 7/12; K. 1/12; L. 3/10; M. 5/14; N. 11/18, O. 2/5; 1,218,375

Page 18
A. 3/10, 5/24, 1/6, 1/12; B. 3/10, 7/15, 5/12, 11/20; C. 17/28, 19/30, 7/18, 1/6; D. 1/35, 1/14, 13/24, 4/15; E. 17/40, 11/21, 7/18, 2/15

Page 19
A. 3 2/5, 1 1/7, 2 1/5, 1 1/6; B. 4 1/3, 4 1/2, 2 1/4, 3 3/10, 1 3/11; C. 3 1/2, 3 1/2, 4 1/4, 5 3/7, 2 1/8; D. 6 7/12, 6 1/4, 4 1/9, 5 1/2, 2 1/12; 5 1/3 − 1 5/6 = 3 1/2 feet deep

Page 20
Because you don't owe or have to pay anything back at the end of the problem!

Page 21
E. 5 1/2; I. 2 1/2; T. 1 3/5; A. 5 4/7; L. 2 3/4; W. 1 2/3; E. 4 4/5; L. 3 2/5; T. 4 2/3; C. 1 2/5 ; N. 1 4/7; G. 2 4/5; S. 3 4/7; M. 5 5/6; J. 7 4/7; WILLAMETTE

Page 22
A. 1 1/5, 2, 1 3/4, 3 1/3; B. 2, 1/2, 4, 3; C. 3 3/4, 5/6, 2, 6; D. 4 1/5, 3, 1 1/2, 3 1/3; E. 4 2/3, 2/3, 4 1/2, 1 3/4; 8 x 3/4 = 6 boxes

Page 23
A. 1/9, 2/5, 3/8, 1/12; B. 1/30, 1/4, 1/6, 1/4; C. 1/4, 1/16, 1/50, 1/18; D. 1/5, 1/12, 1/6, 5/12; E. 3/14, 1/20, 1/8, 1/2; F. 3/10, 4/9, 1/18, 3/14;

200 inches or 508 centimeters

Page 24
3, cowhand; 1 2/7; 1 3/10; 7/10, bookworm; 2, boardwalk; 1 2/5; 1 5/8; 1/4, housefly; 1 1/7; 2, toenail; 2/3, carpool; 4/15, cowboy

Page 25
A. 21, 14, 8, 32, 12; B. 15, 9, 27, 6, 8; C. 15, 6, 2, 30, 12; D. 16, 18, 10, 20, 12; 865,000

Page 26
A. 0.2, 0.5, 0.8, 0.4; B. 0.75, 0.375, 0.6, 0.875; C. 0.2, 0.25, 0.3, 0.25; D. 0.12, 0.5, 0.35, 0.36; E. 0.7, 0.625, 0.9, 0.6; Jack ate 0.125. Lee ate 0.375. Tyler ate 0.5. Yes.

Page 27

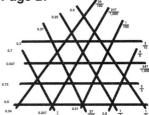

Page 28

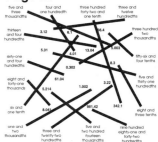

Page 29
0.4, I; 0.6, only; 0.2, want; 0.5, one; 0.1, tenth; 0.9, of; 0.7, that; 0.8, cracker; 0.3, in; 5.7, your; 8.3, hand

Page 30
A. 3.54; B. 56.72; C. 0.98;
D. 24.02; E. 304.03;
F. 75.13; G. 843.06;
H. 89.22; I. 131.71; J. 0.69;
K. 52.32; L. 400.57;
M. 27.04; N. 48.03;
O. 14.62; P. 786.02;
Q. 445.64; R. 625.54;
S. 928.24; T. 4.9

Page 31
A. 1.169; B. 32.006;
C. 9,357.1; D. 7.384;
E. 46.334

Page 32

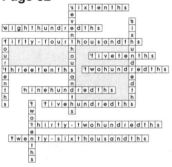

Page 33
<, >, <, <; >, =, >, =; =, >,
>, >; >, <, <, <; >, <, <, >;
<, >, <, >; <; NEITHER!
THEY'RE BOTH EQUALLY
3.575 POUNDS!

Page 34
A. 4.2, 4.4, 4.8, 4.9, MATH;
B. 7.0, 7.3, 7.7, 7.9;
MODE; C. 0.2, 0.3, 0.5,
0.8, GRID; D. 1.9, 3.6, 5.7,
8.4, AREA; E. 2.16, 2.47,
2.89, 2.98, CUBE; F. 0.59,
3.93, 6.48, 8.42, FACE; G.
0.409, 4.09, 6.409, 6.904,
MEAN;
H. 0.92, 3.92, 4.06, 6.9,
LINE; I. 1.8, 4.84, 5.45,
9.08, INCH; J. 1.248,
1.482, 1.824, 1.842, FLIP;
K. 0.59, 5.09, 9.005, 9.05,
TERM

Page 35
A. 2.2 = 2, 3.4 = 3, 4.1 =
4, 5.2 = 5; 2.6 = 3, 2.9 =
3, 3.7 = 4, 4.5 = 5, 4.9 =
5, 5.8 = 6; 6.1 = 6, 6.4 = 6,
7.2 = 7, 7.4 = 7, 8.2 = 8,
9.1 = 9, 9.3 = 9; 6.5 = 7,
7.9 = 8, 8.5 = 9, 9.8 = 10;
B. 5.14 = 5.1, 5.23 = 5.2,
5.31 = 5.3, 5.34 = 5.3, 5.44
= 5.4; 5.15 = 5.2, 5.19 =
5.2, 5.28 = 5.3, 5.38 = 5.4,
5.49 = 5.5; 7.42 = 7.4, 7.51
= 7.5, 7.64 = 7.6, 7.72 =
7.7; 7.45 = 7.5, 7.48 = 7.5,
7.55 = 7.6, 7.69 = 7.7, 7.75
= 7.8, 7.78 = 7.8

Page 36
A. 0.19, 0.62, 0.54, 0.85,
0.65, 0.66, 0.33, 0.91,
0.69, 0.75; Order: 0.19,
0.33, 0.54, 0.62, 0.66,
0.69, 0.75, 0.85, 0.91;
B. 6.42, 5.91, 4.26, 3.69,
5.35, 4.18, 3.15, 6.55,
7.31, 9.43; Order: 3.15,
3.69, 4.18, 4.26, 5.35,
5.91, 6.42, 6.53, 7.31, 9.43

Page 37
A. 3.00 + 2.36 = 5.36, 0.6
+ 0.3 = 0.9, 6.4 + 3.8 =
10.2, 1.32 + 3.21 = 4.53,
8.4 + 2.134 = 10.534; B.
3.04 + 2.06 = 5.10, 0.8 +
0.4 = 1.2, 0.7 + 7.4 = 8.1,
0.43 + 3.41 = 3.84, 6.4 +
1.3 = 7.7; C. 3.4 + 2.3 =
5.7, 6.14 + 1.23 = 7.37,
2.341 + 0.153 = 2.494,
1.34 + 7.14 = 8.48, 1.312 +
2.416 = 3.728

Page 38
A. 0.203 + 6.2 + 7.06 =
13.463, 1.048 + 34.218
+ 3.214 = 38.480, 1.003
+ 2.14 + 26.31 = 29.453;
B. 21.04, + 0.243 + 0.246
= 21.529, 0.343 + 7.06
+ 8.141 = 15.544, 21.04
+ 1.048 + 0.246 = 22.334;
C. 13.102 + 34.218 + 7.06
= 54.380, 0.343 + 0.246
+ 1.003 = 1.592, 21.04
+ 0.203 + 26.31 = 47.553;
D. 34.218 + 1.003 + 2.14
= 37.361, 8.141 + 1.003
+ 0.246 = 9.390, 1.048 +
3.214 + 0.203 = 4.465;
E. 0.243 + 21.04 + 7.06 =
28.343, 13.102 + 34.218
+ 6.2 = 53.520, 23.142,
+ 21.04 + 3.214 = 47.396;
F. 26.31 + 34.218 + 7.06 =
67.588, 23.142 + 1.048
+ 8.141 = 32.331, 0.246
+ 21.04 + 3.214 = 24.500,
1.048 + 0.343 + 2.14 =
3.531

Page 39

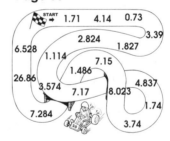

0.79 minutes

Page 40

Page 41
I. 8.4, E. 106.0, A. 229.6,
T. 102.05, W. 2.16, O.
0.32; H. 18.36, S. 2,400.8,
I. 148.86, T. 123.0, I.
124.5, M. 2.080; T. 364.8,
M. 145.5, C. 13.59,
N. 12.32, A. 24.43,
A. 62.46; IT WAS A
MOTH-EMATICIAN.

Page 42

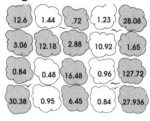

17.28 minutes

Page 43
0.72, 0.018, 0.0024;
0.0015, 0.007, 0.0012,
0.0036; 0.03, 0.002,
4.02, 0.016, 0.0072; 0.98,
0.0012, 8.408, 0.052,
0.0018; 24

Page 44
U. 2.16; L. 36.4; S. 1.56;
Y. 6.47; H. 4.7; R. 0.58;
E. 89.1; M. 6.78; D. 0.89;
A. 0.59; N. 36.8; I. 26.8;
SIR EDMUND HILLARY

Page 45
B. 2.04; L. 0.24; Y. 2.50;
A. 3.05; A. 4.8; K. 6.01;
I. 0.36; S. 5.06; A. 2.08;
U. 0.69; T. 0.58; L. 3.09;
A. 1.06; Y. 1.056; A. 6.07;
LITUYA BAY, ALASKA

Page 46
A. 3.2, 5.775, 0.6625,
3.375, 0.56; B. 0.82, 1.75,
1.75, 3.375, 2.225; C. 7.75,
3.05, 1.6, 2.875, 1.36;
D. 1.12, 1.48, 0.75, 5.625,
0.2625; 0.75 minutes